Head and Heart

My Life in Credit Unions

Tributes

"*Jim's vision and leadership have been essential to the development of Western CUNA Management School as one of the premier educational opportunities available in the credit union movement. Jim's knowledge and passion have filled the hearts and minds of thousands of credit union leaders, making us all better off and the movement even stronger.*" Bill Cheney, former CUNA & Affiliates President/CEO

"*In my opinion, Jim has positively impacted the lives of more credit union members than anyone in the history of the credit union movement.*" Barry Jolette, former CUNA and World Council of Credit Unions board chairman

"*Jim Likens was the right person at the right time, the right place, with the skills to have made a monumental difference to credit union management education. He will be retiring but never forgotten.*" Rick Craig ('81), President/CEO of America First Federal Credit Union (retired)

"*Jim Likens is a brilliant academic leader and has been the heart and soul of WCMS. He has an amazing ability to inspire disparate individuals, mold them into cohesive groups, and motivate them to achieve lofty individual and collective goals.*" David Chatfield, former President/CEO of the California and Nevada Credit Union Leagues (retired)

"*We have all heard of standing on the shoulders of giants to reach new heights. Dr. Jim Likens has provided sturdy shoulders upon which thousands of us have stood— unsteadily at first! Now we too have strong shoulders and can support others.*" Richard Myles Johnson ('74), President/CEO of Western Corporate Federal Credit Union (retired)

"*I have had the honor to know, work, and learn from Jim for nearly 25 years. The impact he has had on the credit union system is immeasurable. His legacy will endure for years through the thousands of students that have graduated from WCMS.*" Diana Dykstra ('92), President/CEO of the California and Nevada Credit Union Leagues

"You can be very proud of the journey you've taken through poverty, austerity, personal success, and service to others. The lives you've touched and elevated along the way by instilling what you've learned over the years are literally countless." Steve Punch, former President/CEO of Jim Likens' credit union, First City Credit Union

"Thank you for the tremendous gift you have given to so many, for your leadership, for your inspirational mentorship and for your friendship." Bill Birnie ('04), President/CEO, Pacific Marine Credit Union

"While WCMS changed my life, it was Jim Likens who helped me find my voice and use it to advance my career, benefit my credit union and impact the credit union industry. Even early on, when I first met Jim, he was much more than my instructor. He quickly became a friend, coach, and mentor." Patsy VanOuwerkerk ('82), President/CEO, Travis Credit Union (retired)

"Over the decades you have meant so much to countless people, but especially to me. As a wise leader, economist, and mentor, you have been a great influence in my life. Thank you for being such a special and remarkable man!" Shruti Miyashiro, President/CEO, Orange County's Credit Union

"My favorite memory of Dr. Likens was how he greeted the incoming class during orientation. The newbies would come in quietly, but by the time Dr. Likens was done they were thoroughly indoctrinated... or maybe mesmerized. It was a wonder to behold!" Molly Davis, former Director of WCMS School Administration (retired)

"I have been told that I am loved many times. But hearing it from you in a room full of people, and believing it, had a huge impact." Kendra Edlin ('17), Education and Community Development Manager, School Employees Credit Union of Washington

"It amazes me that in such a short period of time one individual can touch and shape people's lives, so much so as to even redirect the path we are taking in life, in our careers, and simply as human beings." Vanessa Broemeling ('17), Marketing Manager, Potlatch #1 Federal Credit Union

"I will be eternally grateful to Dr. Jim for the most incredible life-changing experience I have ever had. WCMS changed my life and my career. An incredible teacher and mentor, he brings the fairy dust that allows the students to create the magic." Brandi Gleason ('13), Project Manager, CUNA Mutual

Head and Heart

My Life in Credit Unions

James D. Likens

Woodwind Press
Claremont, California

Head and Heart: My Life in Credit Unions

Also by James D. Likens:
Dust Bowl Grit: A Lifelong Lesson in Dignity and Grace
My Pomona College: A Memoir

Woodwind Press, Claremont CA
ISBN 978-0-692-95109-5

In Memory of Donald Crawford
WCMS Xi Class of '92

Acknowledgments

Michael Steinberger

Steve Punch

Bill Adler

Bill Birnie

Matt Stephenson

David Chatfield

Barry Jolette

Pete Crear

Dick Ensweiler

Diana Dykstra

Rick Craig

Shruti Miyashiro

Carol Payne

Natalie Moreno

Mark Klinkert

Nicolas Nelson

Contents

Preface

Writing this short book has brought back a flood of memories about so many things I have been allowed to do in my passion for credit unions, and about the thousands of people I have known and loved along the way.

For most of my childhood my family lived in poverty. Preparing this remembrance has also reminded me that by the grace of others much good fortune has come to me.

In America, I got to become a professor and teach at one of the finest colleges in the world. In America, I got to become immersed in our fabulous credit union movement. In America, I got to help shape Western CUNA Management School into one of the most important credit union institutions in the country.

When I retired, many of my former students and colleagues sent me congratulatory messages. What an outpouring of love they bestowed. Their messages are beautiful and have touched me deeply. I have agreed to share some of them with my readers in the Tributes, found in the very front of this book.

You will also find plenty of my own tributes to others crowding the pages of this entire book, including its closing chapter.

Gratitude, then, serves both to begin and to bring closure to this book.

I'm grateful to you, too, for reading it.

—Jim Likens, 12 September 2017

Rooted in the Credit Union Cause

My father became an orphan in Iowa at age twelve with no family willing to take him in and no education past eighth grade. My mother graduated from a tiny high school in Oklahoma hoping to become a teacher, but in the Great Depression of the 1930s she could not afford college.

Dad and Mother met and married in rural Arkansas, and shortly after joined tens of thousands of dispossessed people in the great Dust Bowl migration to the Promised Land—California. My first home was a farm labor tent in the Weedpatch Camp outside Bakersfield, California.

My sisters and I were welfare babies, born at government expense at Kern General Hospital. The locals scornfully thought of people like us as Okies.

Dad was a farm laborer. Through much of my childhood our family lived in poverty.

Mother eventually attended the local colleges, and as I was starting seventh grade in 1949 she became a third-grade schoolteacher. Over a period of four years Dad constructed our house—without power tools—and then in 1953, when I was a junior at Bakersfield High School, he became a janitor at my school.

It was then that Dad and Mother discovered Kern Schools Federal Credit Union. At the time it was located on the campus of Bakersfield High School. Dad and Mother had been fearful of banks. Those were for well-heeled people; banks, my parents believed, would not want anyone like them as customers. They got their loans from finance companies.

Kern Schools Federal Credit Union made a big difference in my parents' life. The interest rates were attractive. The service was personal. Dad was very proud that Bill Downs, the manager of the credit union, knew his name. Dad told me that he could get a loan and all he had to do was sign his name, and that his shares would double and his debt would be wiped out if he died. My first car loan was at the credit union, with Dad cosigning.

Years later Vince Rojas, eventually the President/CEO of a now much larger Kern Schools Credit Union, nevertheless knew all the members of my family. When Dad died at age 96, a representative of Kern Schools attended his funeral. The $80,000 Dad proudly willed to my sisters, Ann and Sally, and to me, had been held in a CD account at the credit union. Imagine that he could have accumulated $80,000! My share went to help pay off my daughter's college student loan.

My parents and I realized that education was the best way of escaping poverty and finding a fulfilling life. I received a BA in economics and an MBA in management from the University of California at Berkeley and improbably—while ignoring Dad and Mother's heartfelt advice to get married instead—I took a Ph.D. in economics from the University of Minnesota. For forty-six years, I enjoyed a career as a professor of economics at Pomona College. For forty-three years, I directed the credit union system's highly regarded Western CUNA Management School.

Along the way, I performed other credit union work. I taught thousands of students, published and presented at professional credit union meetings, did consulting and facilitated strategic planning sessions, served on boards of directors, testified as an expert witness in legal cases, and even lobbied successfully in the U.S. Congress.

My parents' discovery of Kern Schools Credit Union when I was a teenager left its impact on me. That memory, and the recognition of the wonderful difference that the credit union made in my parents' lives, was part of my attraction and, ultimately, dedication to serve credit unions as a life's work.

Western CUNA Management School

"In that sweet moment, the princess kissed the little frog prince... Nothing will ever be the same again."　Jim Likens

In 1972, three years after starting as an economics professor at Pomona College, I heard a knock on my office door. It was Bob Voelkel, a respected professor of religion at the College.

He had come to invite me to teach in a summer conference for a credit union management school. The school—by then ten years old—-was moving to Pomona from UCLA, and Bob had been chosen by Pomona to direct it. I agreed to offer some courses. Three years later, when Bob became Vice President and Dean of the College, he recommended me to be his successor.

I will always remember what Damon Roemer—a credit union CEO, who was a member of the school's steering committee—asked me during my job interview: "Do you plan ahead or are you one of those last-minute people?" The truth was I had very little experience running anything, and I didn't know much about time management. But I did know how to answer that question. I told them I planned ahead.

I was invited to begin directing the school in 1975. Today it is called Western CUNA Management School (WCMS). When I accepted the role I had no idea what lay ahead. Between 1934, when the Federal Credit Union Act was passed, and 1975, credit unions remained very simple organizations. Congress and the regulators told them what they could sell, to whom they could sell it, and what price could be charged. It was enough to be competent at operations.

Most credit unions were small and a sophisticated set of professional credit union executives was not yet in place. Dick Heins of CUNA Mutual told me that bankers were not concerned about the success of credit unions; they were not going to outgrow the limitations of their management. Beginning in 1978—as I was getting increasingly involved—everything began coming apart because of inflation, deregulation, and technological innovation. Credit unions had to adapt or die, and I became part of their rapid adaptation.

Students from thirteen Western states attend WCMS each summer for two weeks over a three-year period. They live in the dormitories of Pomona College and take their meals in its dining halls. That structure has not changed, but over time the financial world changed and WCMS changed with it.

I worked to create a WCMS culture that embraces high academic standards while emphasizing credit union philosophy (credit unions are member-owned, not-for-profit cooperatives). That took time. Today WCMS has become one of the premiere credit union organizations in the nation.

I inherited a frog mascot from a carryover UCLA faculty member, psychologist Mario Conforti. A bestselling book, *I'm OK, You're OK*, served him as a practical guide for transactional analysis. People get to choose between warm fuzzies (hugs) and cold pricklies (snubs). Our frog stood for warm fuzzies. What was I to do with this?

I began enhancing that classic story about the prince who offends a witch. Remember? She turns him into a frog and the only way he can become a prince again is to receive a kiss of love from a princess. Head and heart. The prince/frog knows what is required: a kiss. But he cannot simply call out, "Hey, Princess. Listen to me. I am a prince trapped inside this little frog body. Good news. I can offer you beautiful jewels, plus a yacht and a castle. How about a kiss?"

No!

He must of course use his head, plan carefully, carry out his wisest strategy to win her heart—yet in the end his fate rests in her heart, not his plans. She must feel her kiss as an expression of love.

The moral of the story? We are all of us like the little frog prince: we need affirmations of love from others. We are also like the princess: we have the capacity to love others.

An old stereotype of a banker is someone who is all head and no heart. The corresponding stereotype of a credit union person is someone who is all heart and no head. I maintain that for credit union people to be successful we must combine head and heart. Indeed, head and heart are equally important. Credit unions are not just part of a credit union industry. They are organized into a national and international credit union movement. We credit union people are part of something bigger than our individual selves. Let's learn how to combine head and heart for the greater good.

First Year Class Dress for Success: I am Front Row Left Side. August 1975

I oversaw the emergence of a premier management school for credit union professionals featuring highly concentrated academic training. This included fashioning a comprehensive curriculum, with stringent testing and comprehensive projects, and gaining certification for college credit from the American Council on Education. At the same time, an entire culture was being shaped at WCMS that championed noble values and hard work while never neglecting the joy of festivity and fun. These included service-learning activities and communal rituals to foster confident identity, bonding, and teamwork. I intentionally

8

championed self-development, empowerment, group cohesion and cooperation, as well as celebrations of well-earned recognition.

This was my vision of "head and heart," human powers of intellect and compassion conjoined, liberated, and transformational.

To complement the head part of a rigorous academic program one important cultural expression of credit union heart that emerged is service learning: group activities with fund raising that can provide scholarships for others. Everyone comes together to raise money for a good cause. For example, students sometimes organize a welcome walk. A golf tournament. A silent auction. And each of the three classes plans and produces a social event to be enjoyed by everyone. At the graduation ceremony, the graduating students proudly donate their accumulated funds to the school. The class social events are creative and happy. Often, they involve a theme. I very much enjoyed dressing up in support. One was a Howdy Hop dance after a high school football game. I went as the quarterback. Another time I danced as a backup member of the Supremes while Paul Bonnel lip-synced "Stop in the Name of Love." And so many more over the years! What fun!

This WCMS program has enhanced the careers of thousands of credit union professionals and advanced the progress of their credit unions. It has helped produce a generation of credit union leaders deeply committed to credit union principles and to their abiding success.

Bill Birnie, chosen by his class to be their graduation speaker in 2004, said it well: "If you wonder where tomorrow's credit union leaders will come from, look around. They are sitting in this hall tonight."

Tomorrow's Credit Union Leaders

Some of My WCMS Notables

Herein I single out for recognition a few of the colleagues I worked with and who significantly advanced my credit union service. I risk disappointing by omission many other dear friends and colleagues who have played such major parts of my credit union world. Please understand. There are so many of you who have touched my life, and I deeply appreciate your love and support. For a fuller listing, no doubt also regrettably incomplete, I offer a Remembrances chapter at the end of this memoir.

Steven O. Barden

Steven O. Barden

Steve Barden was my first credit union mentor—he got me started in credit unions. Steve was director of education at the California Credit Union League when WCMS moved from UCLA to Pomona College. For many years he chaired the steering committee of WCMS.

He became President/CEO of what today is called First City Credit Union. The Claremont Colleges fall within the field of membership of First City, and Steve persuaded his directors to invite me onto his board. He also taught me about the history and culture of credit unions.

Steve was the son of Lance Barden, a legendary credit union figure. Lance was a federal credit union regulator who also founded over four hundred credit unions. Indeed, it is no exaggeration to say that Steve's father was instrumental in developing the credit union movement in the United States. Like father like son, Steve made credit unions his life's work. His family did the same. His wife Shirley was a credit union CEO. So was his daughter Sue. Daughters Annie and Cindy also worked for credit unions as did Steve's granddaughter Sarah.

Credit unions were in his blood. Steve was chairman of the board of WCMS. I became the President/CEO. Steve and I worked together in these twin capacities for 36 years. The school continues as his and my shared legacy. Each July more than 300 up and coming credit union leaders arrive at Pomona College for the next session of the school. One of them will be attending on a Stephen O. Barden Memorial Scholarship; it will be awarded annually in perpetuity.

Barry Jolette

In 1965 Barry Jolette began nineteen years of unusually dedicated and effective service at the National Credit Union Administration, which regulates federally chartered credit unions and provides deposit insurance for both federal and state chartered credit unions.

Barry Jolette

In July 1987 Barry left federal service to become CEO of San Mateo Credit Union. Soon after, he became involved in the El Camino chapter of the California Credit Union League (CCUL) and in 1996 he served as Chairman of CCUL's Board.

In 1997 Barry was elected to the national CUNA Board, subsequently appointed to serve on its major committees, and then elected to represent CUNA as a delegate to the World Council of Credit Unions. He ended his service on the CUNA Board by serving two years as its Chairman from 2001 to 2003.

Barry served as a Trustee for Western CUNA Management School (WCMS) for more than a decade. During most of that time, he chaired the Budget Committee and also served as the Chairman of the Board. In my role as the school's President and CEO, I had the opportunity to work with Barry and to witness him in action. He was relaxed, consultative, and easy going on the one hand, but committed, resolute, and thorough on the other hand. No job was too big or too small. He paid close attention, but he did not smother. It is no accident that the ascension of WCMS into one of the great organizations of the US credit union movement occurred during Barry's time of participation on our board.

I first met Barry in the early 1980s when he worked in San Francisco as regional director of NCUA. My credit union's attorney Joe Melchione and I called on Barry, asking for permission to merge my credit union with another in an attempt to dig them both out of a financial hole created by unexpected OPEC-induced inflation and the financial disintermediation that followed. The local examiner had recommended against the merger. Other NCUA minions agreed. But Barry listened to our case, sized us up, and to my amazement approved the merger. On the spot! The whole thing took about fifteen minutes! I will never forget it. This was not the behavior of a risk-averse bureaucrat trying to keep his record free of mistakes. This was Barry Jolette, a man of courage and conviction acting in the best interest of credit unions. Thanks to his decision, by the way, we were able to save the combined credit union and today it flourishes.

As previously discussed, students at Western CUNA Management School engage in fundraising activities and proudly donate the proceeds to the school for scholarships. Occasionally this creates a financial hardship for an individual from a small credit union. So each year I made it my business to inquire discreetly whether anyone was strapped for personal money and might feel the embarrassment of not being able to participate. If there was such a person, I quietly telephoned Barry Jolette. He sent money for them— out of his own pocket, anonymously of course.

In 1997 Barry was awarded the California Credit Union League's Distinguished Service Award. In 2003 came the California Credit Union League Presidents Award. In 2005 he received the California Credit Union League's top distinction—the Leo H. Shapiro Lifetime Achievement Award. In 2007 I had the honor of nominating Barry for the nation's top prize: the Herb Wegner Lifetime Achievement Award—and he was selected. I could think of no one in our movement more deserving of that honor.

Subsequently, Barry Jolette was awarded the World Council of Credit Unions' Distinguished Service Award, the global credit union industry's highest honor.

A perpetual scholarship to Western CUNA Management School has been established in his name.

Richard Myles Johnson

Dick Johnson, as CEO of WesCorp, on numerous occasions would telephone me. "Jim, I need your help." Once it was to put on some seminars about the Federal Reserve for top leaders at CUNA, state credit union leagues, and corporate credit unions. At other times he wanted me to speak at one of his conferences, or to present at an environmental task force he had just organized comprised of prominent credit union presidents. I always thought I was doing what he asked: helping him. Of course, it was the other way around. He was mentoring me, giving me exposure and experience with the leaders of the credit union movement so I could participate more fully. Along the way, we became close friends.

Richard Myles Johnson

I was dazzled by his background. Dick Johnson's first career was as a Marine. He fought in three wars, served at the Pentagon, and spent a decade in overseas assignments including three years as an attaché in the U.S. embassy in Taiwan. He was fluent in Chinese.

Dick was a credit union legend who stands as one of the most significant figures in the history of the US credit union movement. The National Credit Union Foundation honored him with the 2002 Herb Wegner Memorial Lifetime Achievement award in recognition of his long and distinguished credit union career.

I am especially proud of Dick's connection to Western CUNA Management School. He graduated from WCMS in 1974 and for fourteen years served as a member of the school's faculty directing Project I. He was the recipient of the first James D. Likens Alumni Recognition Award. He spoke twice at WCMS graduation and also appeared as a speaker in the WCMS series on credit union philosophy, now named in his honor: The Richard Myles Johnson Colloquium in Credit Union Philosophy.

He showed me how to face fear and live bravely with integrity. Shortly before he died he invited me to his home. He didn't say it outright, but we both knew we were saying goodbye. I went to his funeral in July 2016. He was one of the special friends of my life.

Rick Craig

I met Rick Craig in 1979 when he enrolled as a student in WCMS. Like many who attend this school, we saw him as an up-and-comer. Little did we know the extent of his promise. I dropped in to check up and observe his first-year class and was surprised to see Rick, a student, at the blackboard. He was teaching financial analysis to his fellow students. He wrote his contact information on the blackboard and invited them all to call him throughout the upcoming year if they needed any help completing their required credit union projects. I remember thinking we need to get him through this school so he can join the faculty. As soon as he graduated I did invite him to become a member of the faculty of WCMS where he served without interruption for thirty-one years until his retirement in July 2012.

Rick Craig

When I first met him he was second-in-command at America First Credit Union in Utah. He spent his last twelve years as its CEO and was one of the credit union movement's most influential political advocates in both Utah and the United States.

Rick left an indelible mark on WCMS. Between each of the three years of the program students complete Project I and Project II, which analyze their credit unions. Rick became the coordinator of Project II. Rick asked students to send their Project II to him. He read

18

them all, eighty to a hundred projects each year, and wrote extensive comments. Then he sent each student a letter to summarize his assessment of their work and to encourage them.

He invented what came to be known as the "big circle" methodology for large-group discussion.

In addition Rick came across a financial simulation that was out of date so he rewrote the computer code to make it fresh and vital. He then used the model to teach highly evaluated multiple day financial simulations.

Rick didn't just come and teach a few classes like the rest of the faculty and then go home. Year after year— for thirty-two summers—he came and he stayed the entire two weeks. He was crucial to our success.

Rick has a warm human touch. He can talk comfortably with everyone, from entry-level tellers to US Senators.

In 2013 he received the Herb Wegner Lifetime Achievement Award.

He is my dear friend. My wife Chris and I spent many hours of special time in friendship with Rick and his beloved wife Karen before she died in July 2017.

Diana Dykstra

Diana Dykstra enrolled as a student at WCMS as a member of middle management at The Golden 1 Credit Union. She graduated in 1992 with high honors. "I found my voice at WCMS," she was later to say. Following WCMS she was promoted to Senior Vice President at The Golden 1. After a time as Senior Vice President of Patelco Credit Union she became President/CEO of Coast Hills Federal Credit Union and then President/CEO of San Francisco Fire Credit Union.

Diana Dykstra

During this time, Diana served in a volunteer role as chairman and board member of the California Credit Union League. She began teaching at WCMS in 1997. Her principal responsibility that year was coordinating all the moving parts of Project I.

Deeply involved in credit union political advocacy, in 2010 she became the President/CEO of the California and Nevada Credit Union Leagues. That same year she joined the board of trustees of WCMS.

She and Rick Craig became my trusted counsel. Each January the three of us got together to think about emerging issues in the credit union world. These meetings were invaluable. Since my retirement my dear friend Diana has been serving as President of WCMS.

Dubbed the "Queen of Everything" by our students, Diana is now a force for good in our movement. If WCMS had done nothing else in its history except help Diana grow and develop, I would judge the school a triumphant success.

Martha Andresen Wilder

Martha Andresen Wilder for decades was regarded by many as the best teacher at Pomona College. She specialized in Shakespeare. I invited her to teach at WCMS where she created an amazing all-day session for the first-year class called "Passion, I See, is Catching: Shakespearean Lessons in Effective Communication."

Martha Andresen Wilder

To use Shakespeare during an intense program of business education is unexpected, to say the least, but

21

Martha made it work. For her morning sessions, she chose selected scenes from Shakespeare's plays that demonstrated the power of words to manipulate or demoralize for ill or to appreciate and motivate for good. She always included Henry V's stirring oration to his outnumbered soldiers before the Battle of Agincourt in France. It is an inspired, eloquent appeal that moves a small, fearful English army to achieve one of the greatest victories in military history. They join as a "band of brothers" to defeat against seemingly impossible odds the vast aristocratic French army.

For her afternoon sessions, Martha divided the participants into small groups. She asked them, during their lunch hour and break, to create two brief scenes derived from their own rich credit union experience in the workplace, now imagined as a Shakespearean drama! Scene one demonstrated the attitude and language of base and selfish motivations and failed communication. Scene two repeated the situation, but the attitude and language were drastically altered, this time dramatizing strategies of successful communication in which reason and passion, "head and heart," came together. I used to drop in to watch. Hilarious! Creative! And wonderfully insightful and illuminating for us all. The student evaluations of her day were sensational.

She is the recipient of many teaching awards including seven R.J. Wig Distinguished Teaching Awards at Pomona College and the Robert Foster Cherry Award for Great Teaching, an international award sponsored by Baylor University. She was California Teacher of the Year in 1992. In 2006 Pomona College granted her a

"Lifetime Teaching Award," the only one of its kind in the College's history.

I brought Martha into WCMS for three reasons. First, she taught our students powerful lessons about the effective use of language. Second, many of the students experienced a kind of positive internal shift in how they felt about themselves "I learned about Shakespeare, and I loved it. I didn't know I could do that." Third, I wanted my students to meet and observe Martha, this remarkably elegant woman unlike anyone they (and I) had ever experienced. She retired in 2010.

Joseph Melchione

Joe Melchione was a key WCMS faculty member for more than twenty-five years, teaching business law, corporate law and ethics. Joe's contributions to WCMS went far beyond simply sharing his knowledge of the law with our students. He was an ardent evangelist and defender of the ideals and enduring importance of the credit union movement.

Joseph Melchione

He brought this passion to our students in a truly unique way, engaging them in how to get involved and become part of something bigger than themselves. And he did it all with such style! He would walk into the first year class, an aging hippy, long hair flowing down his back, sporting an Armani suit and expensive shoes. And then he would proceed to profess. A spellbinder. Sometimes when he got himself really worked up, he ranted. "What has happened to our country? Millions of dollars awarded to someone who spilled hot coffee on herself. Outrageous! Crazy! Whatever happened to personal responsibility?"

Joe enthusiastically supported student fundraising endeavors. He found ways to motivate students to take fundraising seriously. I watched in fascination as Joe challenged a brand new class. He promised to let them cut off several inches of his hair if they could raise $2000 before the next break, which was only twenty minutes away. They rose to the challenge, and did. That wasn't all. Joe drew cartoon characters of himself to be sold at auction, and donated other unusual things. My favorite: he once donated a pair of his new Godzilla boxer underwear for that evening's auction event. The bidding was furious, I remember, and something came over me. That night I reached into my deep pockets and outbid everyone. Yes, I bought Joe Melchione's Godzilla underwear at an outrageous premium. A collector's treasure, wouldn't you agree?

The WCMS credit union students adored Joe. We all did. His legacy is that he helped educate an entire generation of credit union leaders. He died in 2012. I spoke at his funeral. Joe's partners at Styscal, Wiese and

Melchione have established a perpetual scholarship in his memory.

Michael Steinberger

Michael is my successor at WCMS. During my last ten years as President & CEO he served as the school's Dean. Michael is one of my closest friends; I was a groomsman at his wedding. He has it all: intellect, passion and character. He is gifted.

Michael graduated from the University of California at Berkeley with three majors: Economics, Political Science, and Statistics. He received Highest Honors in each of them, was awarded the Department Citation Award in Statistics, and was admitted to Phi Beta Kappa as a Junior. He earned a Ph.D. in Economics from one of the very best economics departments in the world, at the Massachusetts Institute of Technology.

Michael Steinberger

Michael is widely acclaimed among students for the enthusiasm, drive and humor he brings to the classroom. In his very first year of eligibility, in May 2008, Michael was awarded the R.J. Wig Distinguished Professor Award for Excellence in Teaching, Pomona College's highest honor for exceptional teaching, concern for students, and service to the College and community. Eight years later in his second year of eligibility in 2016 he won again. Michael is equally popular as a teacher with our WCMS students. The school is in good hands!

Bill Broxterman

Sherlock Holmes famously solved the case of a stolen racehorse by noting that the stable's guard dog had chosen not to bark as the theft was occurring. By not barking, the dog conveyed a message—the thief was an insider.

I suggest that WCMS was altered for the good because of something that Bill Broxterman, Chairman of the California League, did not do. As the school began to succeed, Bill could have attempted to have his California League take it over. He could have tried to capture the school and make it part of his organization. He did not do so. To his credit, Bill seems to have recognized that by letting WCMS stay in the hands of academicians and influential credit union CEOs and league presidents, who volunteered for the job, he was doing what was best for credit unions and—ultimately—his California league. Bill allowed his organization to serve as host league while he and

WCMS always made it clear that the school served all of our state associations equally.

Bill Broxterman

The level of trust he made possible was a key to the sustained success of WCMS. Such a gift!

28

Donald Crawford

One of my treasured memories is Diana Dykstra's tribute to Don Crawford—who was the brother I never had—which Diana read at WCMS graduation just after Don died. I share it here in its entirety.

**Don Crawford in Red Shirt with Walkie Talkie,
Diana Dykstra in White T-shirt on Right Side with Walkie Talkie**

A Tribute to Donald Crawford

Diana Dykstra

"He has achieved success who has lived well, laughed often and loved much; who has filled his niche and accomplished his task; who has left the world better than he found it; who has never lacked appreciation of Earth's beauty or failed to express it; who has always looked for the best in others and given them the best he had; whose life was an inspiration; whose memory, a benediction."

Three weeks ago, Don Crawford lost his battle with cancer.

Don and I arrived at WCMS in the summer of 1990, and like all who have come before and after, we were assaulted on all sides by hugs from smiling people in shirts covered with frogs.

That afternoon Don and all of his new classmates were herded into Lyman Hall where we listened intently to gain an understanding of what was about to happen to us.

I can still see it in my mind's eye. I felt pretty apprehensive. Did I really belong here? Who were all these strange people? And when Dr. Likens told us he loved us, I was ready to bolt from the room. Then a quiet voice from behind me muttered "Oh no, not another California touchy-feely thing." I turned and saw Don Crawford for the first time. From that moment, I knew had a friend.

Two years later, Don and I sat side by side on this very stage—because no one came between Crawford and Dykstra! Don graduated with honors that night. His classmates chose him as their commencement speaker, and oh what a speech. If you were there, you remember.

Don talked about the power of WCMS to change lives, his in particular, for Don believed the outpouring of love he received from us during his first encounter with cancer had saved his life.

Who were we to disagree?

Don never left WCMS. He returned in 1993 as a GA, and in 1994 he became the school's director of communications.

Don made an enormous contribution to our school. He has forever changed the look, feel, style—and the ethos—of the WCMS experience.

What I find especially amusing is that in 1993, his first year on the WCMS management team, Don welcomed the first-year students at their Sunday afternoon orientation, and guess what he did? Just like Dr. Likens, he told the students about the love and magic they would find at this school... Don had got it, here at WCMS—head and heart—and he wanted to make sure everyone knew how important the school was to him.

Those of us fortunate enough to have been around WCMS over the last thirteen years could see that Don was an artist.

He of course graced us with creativity and flare in everything he touched, but this was never more evident that when he sang and played guitar for us during Sunday evening concerts—and boy could he work a crowd.

This past February, Don's doctors told him that he was finally losing his battle with cancer. Then came the news that he needed round-the-clock assistance. Don had no long-term health insurance. So we sent out a simple request to our friends for help.

In less than a month, WCMS alumni, faculty, and students poured in nearly $18,000 to pay for his care, and it was clear more money would be available if needed.

Hundreds of cards and letters poured in as well. Don was grateful—but not surprised—and so very touched by the love and caring that his WCMS family provided for him.

He knew this was the magic of WCMS. Don died feeling our love, our admiration, and our appreciation for the blessing of the gift of his life in ours.

In Don's memory, we are donating the remaining $5,000 from the trust for a scholarship that has been created in his name. That is what he would have wanted.

WCMS has many individuals who are immortalized for their significant contributions to the school. Tonight, along with the great names of Charlie Clark and Mario Conforti, we add the name of Donald Crawford.

Political Action

April 1978, when I first joined the board of First City Credit Union, was a crucial time for the economy. Unexpected inflation and high interest rates threatened the very existence of credit unions. Disintermediation of deposits out of credit unions into banks, S&Ls, and new money market funds was leading to severe financial problems for credit unions. Authorized interest rate ceilings imposed by law were held below the unprecedented high market interest rates determined as a consequence of Federal Reserve Chairman Paul Volker's anti-inflation monetary policy. I saw that credit unions were headed for disaster.

At only my second board meeting, I urged us to ask the National Credit Union Administration (NCUA), our federal regulator, to raise its 6% interest ceiling on deposits, and also to call on the US Congress to lift the 12% usury ceiling on loans written into the 1934 Credit Union Act. My new First City board looked at me like I had just stepped off a spaceship from Mars.

I sought out credit union political leadership to make the case. I wound up participating extensively with them in a two-year effort to bring about the necessary changes. This included many speeches at credit union meetings and conferences around the nation. The House Banking Committee reluctantly offered inadequate help and threatened to withdraw it if credit union lobbyists appealed to the Senate.

Bill Broxterman of the California Credit Union League arranged for me to take a small group and meet secretly, against the orders of the House Banking Committee, with Alan Cranston, the Democratic majority leader of the US Senate.

"What will happen if Congress does not lift the 12% ceiling on loans as you are urging?" Cranston asked me.

"You will own federally insured credit unions," I replied. "They will collapse, and NCUA, the federal deposit insurance provider, will have to liquidate them."

Cranston handed me a card with a phone number. "Call my staffer, Julie, tomorrow morning. We will fix this problem in conference," he promised.

They did! It was huge! That one change staved off disaster for federally charted credit unions.

It was Public Law 96-211, March 31, 1980, 94 STAT 132 which included both increased maximum loan rates, and permanent share draft authority.

Service on the National Scene

As I became better known, I enjoyed receiving invitations to speak before credit union audiences at conferences throughout the United States and Canada. I provided forecasts of economic conditions for credit unions. I gave advice and counsel on a wide range of topics such as competition, demographics, technology, history, and cooperative philosophy. I did a lot of this. One week I spoke in Key West, Florida on Tuesday and in Dallas, Texas on Thursday—all the while teaching my Monday, Wednesday, and Friday classes at Pomona College in California.

I also served as an expert witness on behalf of credit unions in a number of legal cases. This included, most notably, a suit against the Franchise Tax Board in California by state-chartered credit unions over the interpretation of an accounting rule that affected imposition of taxation. I was on the witness stand for several days. The state was applying harsh rules that would have crippled state-chartered credit unions. We lost, but confidently appealed to the California Supreme Court. That case became moot because the problem was solved through credit union political advocacy in the state legislature of California.

I was asked to consult widely on strategic planning and economics with individual credit unions. I helped credit unions of all sizes develop strategic plans, become financially solvent, and improve relations between senior management and volunteers. I also proposed and facilitated two significant mergers that improved service to members of both credit unions.

Credit Union Economist

I dedicated much of my professional career to studying credit unions. I have no trouble staying interested. Their world seems constantly to be in a state of flux. Here are some insights and lessons learned over the years.

Deregulation

Ronald Reagan's appointment of Ed Callahan to become NCUA Chairman in October of 1981 could not have come at a better time. The primary issue in the credit union movement was survival. Double digit inflation and short-term interest rates of 12-16% had pushed credit unions to a perilous place.

Prior to this time, the government set the rates, terms, and conditions for all savings accounts and had an unworkable 12% usury ceiling on federally chartered credit union loans. It was government regulators, not the leaders in the credit union, who determined who could be served and what could be sold.

Some relief came in 1977 by way of new laws that allowed credit unions to begin offering new services including mortgage lending and shares certificates.

In the 1980s, credit unions were given more flexible criteria for mergers and field of membership. They were also permitted to offer increased services to members.

Ed famously posted a sign outside his office in Washington DC: "We don't run credit unions." The message announced Ed's approach to supervision. I remember suddenly feeling a wonderful difference in my credit union's interactions with NCUA examiners.

Supported by enabling legislation from the Reagan-era Congress, Ed oversaw three key changes while at the helm of the NCUA: (1) deregulating saving and loan interest rates, (2) allowing a credit union to serve multiple groups, and (3) challenging credit unions to capitalize their own share insurance fund.

Largely as a result of such decisions credit unions have been able to flourish.

After leaving the NCUA, Ed went on to found Callahan & Associates in Washington, DC, which became the leading provider of independent financial data concerning credit unions in the United States.

Ed Callahan and Jim Likens at WCMS

Ed later became CEO of the San Francisco-based Patelco Credit Union.

Ed Callahan saved my credit union. He did it by empowering us to save it ourselves. What a breath of fresh air that was.

I had the pleasure of working with Ed on a WesCorp advisory task force. He also was the featured speaker in 1998 for Philosophy Night at WCMS.

Strategic Market Position

With deregulation in place, credit unions had to come up with their own strategies. I thought about how to address this issue at WCMS. I eventually came to conceive a credit union's strategic market position as the simultaneous decisions it makes about these ten variables:

Field of Membership	Systems
Breadth of Product Line	Technology
Value Added	People
Pricing	Image
Service Quality	Differentiation

These elements can be conceptualized as a ten-dimensional vector moving through time and space, always being adapted and transformed as the world changes. The parts must fit together harmoniously.

This is the framework for the strategic part of the WCMS curriculum.

When Picasso was painting the 11'6" x 25'6" Guernica his task each day was to decide: What to add now? He added line and color every day until he was done. He could have stopped too soon. He could have continued too long. But he knew exactly when his masterpiece was complete.

Picasso's Guernica

When Michelangelo was sculpting his seventeen-foot-tall marble masterpiece of David, his decision each day was: What to remove now? He chiseled and polished away stone until he was done. He could have stopped too soon. He could have continued too long. He knew exactly when to stop and put away his tools.

Michelangelo's David

These are powerful metaphors. Whether we start with positive space and remove elements, or begin with negative space and add them, strategy is the boundary between what we do and what we do not do. Wise leaders will focus here, on these key elements. In my view, a list of one-year and five-year goals and projects is not a strategy. It might, of course, represent an adaptation in strategy in response to changes in the environment.

National Credit Union Capitalization Commission

In the late 1970s, CUNA leadership established a Commission to explore the issue of capitalization. I was invited to participate as a Resource Person.

The Commission set up four groups. One group studied the purposes and forms of capital within credit unions and methods to assure capital growth at the individual credit union level. A second group considered capitalization of the newly forming corporate credit unions. A third group explored the roles and relationships of the credit union system with the Central Liquidity Facility (CLF) and the Federal Reserve System. A fourth group looked at ways capital might be generated to develop new services and support systems.

The Commission submitted its report in May 1982. It was well-received. I believe the report of the Commission helped educate and prepare credit union leaders for the necessity of building capital. It certainly helped me. Looking back at the four Commission studies:

(1) NCUA and state regulators solved the capitalization problem by insisting that credit unions build and maintain adequate capital levels. Return on assets, the capital ratio and the growth of assets are linked by

algebra. Through their assignment of financial ratings during examinations, regulators could insist that credit unions when necessary suppress the growth of assets so as to build up their capital ratios.

(2) Member credit unions agreed to a plan and successfully capitalized the corporate credit unions over time, and this was very well done.

(3) The Central Liquidity Facility (CLF) was created to serve as a liquidity lender to credit unions experiencing unusual or unexpected liquidity shortfalls. Membership by credit unions and corporate credit unions was voluntary and open to all those that purchased a prescribed amount of stock. The president of the CLF managed the facility under the oversight of the NCUA Board. The CLF was important in helping the credit union system deal with the 2008-2010 financial crisis.

(4) As for looking for capital to develop new services and support systems, we do, of course, have a number of valuable credit-union-oriented cooperatives like CU Direct and Co-Op Financial Services that join long-time CUNA Mutual. We have also seen the rise of a plethora of market-based vendors that are available to credit unions, which helps reduce the need for the credit union system to produce support products and services themselves.

Economists and Political Scientists: Who Is in Charge?

Economists see the world as organized around markets. Political scientists think about a world occupied by nation states. The credit union world I first encountered in the 1970s was led by people who thought like political scientists. Members joined Credit

Unions which belonged to local Chapters and to state Leagues. Leagues belonged to CUNA. Ideally, every state would have its own League.

Who was de facto in charge in this world? In the early days of very small credit unions, volunteer directors led their small credit union staffs, and these directors filled leadership positions at chapters and leagues, sometimes all the way to the CUNA board. CUNA was pretty much in charge.

Then came the rise of the league presidents, and for a time they were in charge—actually, a few of the most influential league presidents and the top executives of CUNA were in control.

But then came the rise of the credit union CEOs whose credit unions in some cases commanded more resources than were available to many league presidents and maybe even to CUNA itself.

CEOs of the largest credit unions began to attend roundtable groups organized by the California Credit Union League and by CUNA to discuss emerging issues. They gradually acquired a taste for political influence. The CEOs began to expect a larger voice in the direction of the movement.

So the national movement reorganized its governance system and put CEOs of credit unions on the CUNA board. Today the CUNA board consists of eighteen CEOs and five league presidents and the president of CUNA.

Beginning in the late 1970s the corporate credit unions came on the scene. How would they fit in? Initially the political scientists still had an answer. In their view, in its purest form, every state should have a league, and every state should have a corporate. Note that there were originally forty-two corporate credit unions. All these corporates would do some business through a national credit union, US Central, just like the leagues were expected to interact with CUNA.

But there was some difference of opinion over control of corporates. In some states, the league president was in charge of both the league and the corporate, and in others the corporate had its own independent structure. John Arnold headed up Southwest Corporate in Texas and reported to Jack Eaker, president of the Texas league. Dick Johnson ran WesCorp and did not report to the president of the California league.

A related problem occurred with the corporates. They were meant to offer traditional correspondent wholesale services to retail natural-person credit unions. Here the economies of scale are large, and many of the corporates were too small to be viable. Consolidation was inevitable.

Even though the number of corporates was shrinking, they worked reasonably well when they were offering traditional correspondent banking services like item processing. But an aspect of the corporate business model was flawed.

Credit unions were supposed to place some funds of members in their corporate, which in turn would move some money to US Central, which could invest into the financial markets. But the interest rate spread between what the members earned and what the markets paid was too narrow to support three tiers of credit unions: natural person credit unions, corporates, and US Central.

The largest credit unions sometimes wished to bypass their corporate and go directly to US Central. Others might wish to go to a large corporate like WesCorp and stay there. Both practices violated the sensibilities of the political science crowd. But they made good sense to the economists.

The rules changed in the face of economic reality. Mergers of corporates were allowed, and corporates were permitted to expand nationwide. They did so aggressively—to me it felt like the way I imagine the 1889 Oklahoma land rush. Grow like mad. and take on extra risk in the hope of securing market share. Some of the largest corporate credit unions chased yield by investing in what turned out to be troubled mortgage-backed securities that experienced dramatic, unprecedented declines in value, effectively rendering five of these corporates insolvent including US Central and WesCorp.

NCUA reported on 3 July 2017 that the corporate system has contracted and consolidated, with assets falling from $81 billion in 2010 to $25 billion today. In that same time period, the number of corporates declined from twenty-six to just eleven.

A transformation has also occurred at CUNA and the leagues. In the 1970s when I first got involved with CUNA, the "fifty" leagues hoped to sell operational products and services to credit unions. It was the political science voice at work. The economist's voice said "no" and eventually prevailed.

In recent years there has been a consolidation of leagues—in 2017 there were only thirty-seven with more league mergers to be expected. Credit unions today may join their league or CUNA or both. CUNA and the leagues no longer focus on selling products and services directly to credit unions but offer them through market-based affiliated companies. The leagues and CUNA use dues dollars primarily to focus on traditional trade association activities like political advocacy, compliance, research, and education.

Today, much innovation is coming from organizations like CU Direct and CO-OP Financial Services. CU Direct started at The Golden 1 Credit Union in California. It made it possible for people to buy cars from dealers and at the same time join a credit union to finance their car loan. This program became a partnership between The Golden 1 and the California league. It became a successful cooperative owned by credit unions under the excellent leadership of Tony Boutelle. Today CU Direct is the largest indirect auto lending organization in the United States, surpassing Wells Fargo.

The organization today known as Co-Op Financial Services also started at the California league. It was led by the very competent Bob Rose, followed by visionary Stan Hollen. In 2017 it is providing a very wide range of services to more than half of all credit unions in the United States.

These are examples of entrepreneurship paired with collaboration in a cooperative structure. Political scientists and economists conjoined!

The credit union movement in the United States is dominated by about a thousand credit unions that control 85% of the nation's credit union assets. In my view, this is working very well. Credit unions in America are on a good path.

Economies and Diseconomies of Scale and Scope

The consumer services financial sector is becoming increasingly concentrated—a growing share of total assets is in the hands of the largest players. To understand why this is the case I conducted empirical research to identify the causes and extent and effect of economies and diseconomies of scale and scope in credit unions.

Large asset size, low expense-to-asset ratios, and large average share per member commonly provide the best financial conditions for financial yield and asset growth and financial success. Over-expanding geographically, aggravated by the difficulty of monitoring employee behavior, is a common source of diseconomies of scale. It is also a great advantage to be big enough in one's geographic setting to have a marketing voice, what economists call an economy of scope. It is therefore easier to thrive in medium-sized metro areas than in the very largest cities.

Everywhere credit unions are attempting to grow to attain sufficient scale to survive. The wave of credit union mergers over the past three decades has been driven by economies of scale and scope.

Comparative Economic Systems

I traveled to Australia, New Zealand, English-speaking Canada and French-speaking Canada to study the credit union movements in those places and to contrast them with credit unions in the US. I observed that, though credit unions across the globe are affiliated philosophically through the World Council of Credit Unions, they are affected profoundly by national variations in laws & regulations, competition with other financial entities, population demographics, and cultural variations. So, as financial institutions evolve, they are shaped by the national environments in which they operate. Credit unions across international lines are more like cousins than siblings.

New Zealand does not have deposit insurance, which is used in most advanced countries to prevent runs on banks and financial panics. The government did intervene with deposit insurance during the 2008 financial crisis but removed the program in 2012. I believe it is as a consequence that New Zealand has only 13 credit unions and 180,000 members for a population of 4.693 million people and an anemic consumer real estate market. The system is shrinking.

Credit unions in Australia were denied access to bank clearinghouse services; taxation was the political price they paid to get it. Australian credit unions also do not have deposit insurance, though they do have regulators who watch out for the safety and soundness of depositors' funds. The national government announced its willingness to stand by to intervene during the 2008 financial crisis should that have been necessary. Australia has 91 credit unions and just over 4,000,000 members and the equivalent of $470 billion U.S. dollars in assets.

In contrast, in 1970 the US Congress established the NCUIF, which provides deposit insurance for credit unions. With deposit insurance, the US government makes sure there will never be a panicked run on the credit union by its depositors. The response was immediate. Credit unions grew tremendously during the 1970s, the number of credit union members more than doubling during the decade, and credit union assets tripling to more than $65 billion. Today US credit unions total $1.1 trillion in assets with 112 million members. Deposit insurance brought intrusive examinations by the NCUA and state regulators, but the price was well worth paying.

By the way, NAFCU was formed by large federal credit unions to advocate for deposit insurance. CUNA at the time was dominated by small credit unions that opposed share insurance, fearing intrusive government regulation they expected would follow.

Credit unions throughout Canada have their deposits insured by provincially-established institutions. In French-speaking Quebec credit unions are called Caisses Populaires.

In both Canada and the US, credit union membership and assets are growing while the number of credit unions declines. There are two main reasons for this, one widely reported and the other not.

The first reason is technology, which offers economies of scale and scope (discussed above). Big credit unions have lower operating costs as a percent of assets, which gives them a competitive advantage. The number of credit unions has been falling since the early 1970s as smaller credit unions are forced to shut down or are merged into the larger credit unions that have the economies of scale.

The second reason is labor-force demographics. The best credit union fields of membership serve a strong employment base such as members of the armed forces or teachers or telephone employees or public employees. Companies like Boeing, United Airlines, and Caterpillar also come to mind. But employment in government and in manufacturing is not growing as a fraction of the US labor force. Significantly, the share that is growing is the nongovernmental service sector. It now employs about two-thirds of all American workers. Problematically, the average firm in this sector employs just five hundred people, too small to support an employment-based credit union. Consequentially, community-based credit unions become the only hope for reaching these people, and such credit unions are hard to make successful because it is so difficult to find a marketing voice in the general financial marketplace.

US credit unions enjoy a federal tax exemption and compete vigorously with community banks for Congressional advantage. But both are constrained by the market power of the largest US national banks.

English-speaking Canadian credit unions pay some taxes and occupy a niche similar to that of community banks and the old S&Ls in the US. French-speaking Canadian credit union leaders are willing to surrender local control to central cooperative groups to achieve economies of scale in system-wide technology, whereas English-speaking Canadian and US credit unions are willing to cooperate, but only to a lesser extent.

Canada has 695 credit unions with 10 million members and US$229 billion in assets.

The Origins of Credit Unions

The twentieth century credit union movements of the United States and Canada were based on a formal structure of credit union laws, chartering, legal powers, regulation, contracts, courts, and generally accepted accounting principles.

This has not been the case for credit unions' origins— the informal credit cooperatives that emerged on every continent. Without such a formal complex structure, people from all around the world have simply banded together in informal financial cooperation.

Such associations exist worldwide. They carry such names as *chit funds* in India, *cheetu* in Sri Lanka, *tontines* in Senegal, *njangis* in Cameroon, *su-su* in Jamaica, *cundina* in Mexico, *cuchubal* in El Salvador, *pasanakus* in Bolivia, *kye* in Korea, *tanamoshi* in Japan, and *hui* in Taiwan.

How do they manage without the formal structure of today's credit unions? What significant purposes do they accomplish with this approach?

Imagine a place where no credit bureaus exist that would permit lenders to check the credit history of potential borrowers. Suppose people cannot present potential lenders with paycheck stubs or any other proof of employment and income. Imagine they cannot provide any credible evidence of the amounts of their bills and expenses. How can anyone grant credit to people for whom it is impossible to check credit-worthiness?

Suppose laws and property rights are not well established. Title to property cannot be readily established. The rules for repossessing collateral do not exist. Courts have not been instituted that effectively enforce contracts for consumer loans. Standards for bankruptcy have not yet been created. The very governments that might set up the rules may exploit ordinary people. How can anyone have any confidence that loans can ever be collected?

Clearly, under these circumstances people will find it difficult if not impossible to secure formal credit on reasonable terms from reputable market-based consumer lenders. Credit, if available at all, will be provided informally by family and friends, or through various pawnbrokers, loan sharks, and moneylenders. Family and friends typically do not have enough funds. Moneylenders charge very high interest rates. Such is, and has been for thousands of years, the situation for many people around the world, especially the poor.

But there is an alternative. People can band together through informal cooperative credit associations and provide credit to one another. They can start by pooling their resources cooperatively so long as they know one another well enough to trust that their funds will not be misappropriated. They can also make loans to one another with these funds. For one thing, these neighbors do not have the same limited information about one another as the outsider market-based lenders have about them. With respect to one another, these neighbors are insiders. They speak the same language. They practice the same religion. They share a common culture and a common set of values. They know who among their neighbors is reliable and trustworthy. They know who works hard. They know who keeps commitments. The informal credit associations can personally evaluate the credit-worthiness of their neighbors.

People also have ways to help assure that the loans they make to one another will be paid back. Those who don't repay their loans will lose face. One cannot easily melt away in isolation into another part of the community. If someone defaults on a loan, which neighbor will help him build a house? Who will help sew a quilt? Who will offer a ride to work? Who will agree to play cards at the lodge each Friday evening? Who will allow a son or a daughter to date, let alone marry, the offspring of someone who has betrayed the credit association? Without the help and friendship of neighbors, how can one survive? The informal credit associations have powerful informal means for collecting loans made to their neighbors.

There it is! The origins of our credit union values: Cooperative philosophy. People helping people. The common bond. Very old values, and very effective even in today's modern world.

Today, of course, US credit unions can also operate in an environment that makes it possible to do business at arm's length with strangers. Our challenge is to continue to use those "tools of the head" to serve our "goals of the heart" just as proto-credit unions do.

Wegner Award for Lifetime Achievement

I was granted the Herb Wegner Lifetime Achievement Award in Washington DC on February 27, 2005, at a black-tie dinner attended by more than a thousand people. It is the highest national credit union honor bestowed in the United States. My family was with me, along with many dear credit union friends. In accepting I spoke from my heart. Following the photo is my acceptance speech.

Accepting the Herb Wegner Lifetime Achievement Award
Presented by
Mary Cunningham and Steve Delfin

Whew! What a night! I don't know whether to laugh or cry! I'm absolutely overwhelmed.

First, congratulations to Chris Rosenthal, to the Vermont Development Credit Union, and to Dennis Dollar.

Thank you to the National Credit Union Foundation for this fabulous award, to Chuck Purvis and the foundation's selection committee, and to Kris Hoffman for her many kindnesses.

Thank you John Annaloro and the WA League, for nominating me. My gratitude to all the dear friends who supported my nomination.

I really appreciate the people who found all those pictures, and everyone who produced the video. Kathleen Iattarelli and Stewart at Grassland Media. Bruce Bennett at CUNA Mutual who put it all together. The video is very moving and I will treasure it always.

FROM WCMS

I want to salute the board of trustees of WCMS; Barry Jolette, David Chatfield, Mary Cunningham, Tracie Kenyon, Mark Klinkert, Michael Litzau, Ava Milosevich, Shruti Miyashiro, Bernie Ray, Vince Rojas, Larry Sharp, and Patsy Van Ouwerkerk. Isn't that a fabulous lineup? I wouldn't trade them for any board in the world.

Thanks to all the other wonderful people who have served on the WCMS board in the past, most recently

Dianne Harding, Joe Schroeder, Scott Earl, Gary Plank and Gene Poitras.

Hurrah for the WCMS management team, David Ellings, Molly Davis and Nancy Wood (they are all here).

Cheers to the California League professionals who worked in partnership with me at WCMS over the years: Mark Klinkert, Donna Stone, Tom Vigueras, Bill Sterner, and Ginny Baldauf.

Kudos to the graduate assistants who are selected each year to return to WCMS to help out.

My best to the WCMS alumni association who keep the spirit alive.

I want to honor the memory of Charlie Clark, Mel Silverman, Mario Conforti—great men—and the beautiful Don Crawford, who became the brother I never had.

FROM FIRST CITY CREDIT UNION

The Board: My buddies Chuck Miller, Bruce Palmer, Willa Glover, Jack Preston, Bob Ciulik, Joe Milner—and the memory of Reverend Philip Pitts. Haven't we had some times together? Come out west to First City and visit our board if you want to see it done right. Best practices! Second to none! You're the best!

The First City staff and supervisory committee: These are the folks who put those best practices into practice.

Our gifted CEO, Steve Punch: Steve, thank you for making us successful. Steve is smart. Strategic. Full of integrity. A natural leader. He's the real deal!

I WANT TO MENTION A FEW OTHER SPECIAL PEOPLE

Steve Barden, who is the person who brought me into the movement more than thirty years ago.

Three credit union icons, all Wegner Lifetime Achievement Award winners:

Dick Johnson, my most important and sustaining credit union mentor, the person who introduced me to the national movement. My friend. Dick always gave me the impression I was mentoring him; it took me years to figure out it was really the other way around. I am honored to have Dick sitting at my table tonight.

Bill Broxterman, a giant among us, who from the beginning involved me in critically important credit union work and who, more than anyone else, nurtured my zeal for credit unions.

David Chatfield, a force of nature; how brave and wise he is. Dave always supports me and accepts me as this odd duck combination of CU insider and independent thinker.

The faculty of WCMS over the years, especially Rick Craig and Diana Dykstra.

Vince Rojas and all the good folks at Kern Schools Federal Credit Union who showed my family that we mattered, and helped us find a place of financial security and dignity.

Comrades in arms: Joe Melchione, Gene O'Rourke, and Randy Moore. We've been to the wars together, fighting side by side for good credit union causes. If I'm ever in trouble I hope to God you're still willing to be on my side.

Ed Callahan (another Wegner Award recipient) and Barry Jolette, who during their NCUA days found creative and courageous ways to let First City Credit Union work out its own problems.

The hundreds of credit unions I have worked with over the years, and CUNA and all the leagues that have invited me to give so many programs, presentations and seminars.

STUDENTS

And then there are my WCMS students, past and present: I know some of you are here. Thousands of you around the country hold positions of leadership in our movement. Your careers inspire me. You are my legacy. I am so very proud of you. Don't forget the princess and the little frog prince, and the power of head and heart to transform lives. And hand, too: lend a hand, work hard for our movement. Never give up. You are the future.

MY FAMILY

My family is here tonight: My wife Chris, what a fine person she is. I love you and respect you so much, Chris, with all my heart. Our kids and their spouses are here tonight as well: David and Norma, Andy and Gail, Elizabeth and Christopher; Chris and I call them "the babies." You are so talented and beautiful. How lucky we are that you still want to come home to be with us. And our granddaughter: Victoria Elizabeth Likens ("Snookums") who is six years old. See me later for pictures and brag stories.

MOM AND DAD

You have left this world, but I carry you in my heart.

We had some tough times: a "Grapes of Wrath" migration to California, where I was born during the Great Depression, a welfare baby born at government expense, who went home to a tent in a government labor camp. The people of Kern County didn't want our kind going to school with their children, so the Dust Bowlers had a school of their own in the government camp.

I remember our family getting started. Buying a house in California. Then returning for a disastrous year of trying to farm in Arkansas, and going broke in the effort: returning to California in a broken-down car, living in a tent in a cotton field, with no money, and feeding ourselves by picking cotton for 3 cents a pound.

Up against it. Flat broke. Merle Haggard sings about it. If you've ever been poor you can feel his music deep in your insides: "If we make it through December..." "Tulare Dust." "Mama's Hungry Eyes."

I was asked to provide some photos of this period for the video. Couldn't do it. When you are as poor as we were, you don't have a camera.

It's a miracle that I am here with you tonight.

While Mom picked cotton she was exposed to DDT, which may have given her the ovarian cancer that later killed her. But she also rode the high school bus into Bakersfield and got an emergency credential to teach third grade to the little dust bowl kids in Lamont. Dad worked twelve hours a day in the fields, before becoming a janitor at the high school, and in his spare time he built our house. Brick by brick.

They had the vision to send me to Berkeley. To the University of California. They saw it as a combination of Harvard, Oxford, and Oz. And it was.

Mom and Dad. You never gave up or fell into despair. You always believed in the future, that our life would be better. We always had a dream, a plan, a vision of the future. This is the single most important gift I received from you: Hope & optimism.

Mom and Dad. Thank you. I have always loved you. I hope you are proud of me.

ONLY IN AMERICA

In America, I got to become a professor and teach at one of the finest colleges in the world.

In America, I got to become passionately immersed in our fabulous credit union movement.

In America, I got to help shape Western CUNA Management School into one of the most important credit union institutions in the country.

In the 1970s a young Dick Heins told me that bankers were not afraid of credit unions. Credit unions were not going to outgrow the limitations of their management. Now bankers are suing us. Turns out our management is pretty good after all. And through WCMS I have had the privilege of helping shape a generation of credit union leaders. It is profoundly satisfying to me— profoundly satisfying—that my credit union students, thousands of them, have earned their places in the ranks of professional CU management all across America.

I think that Herb Wegner is looking down on us right now, and that he is smiling, because his beautiful credit union movement is in good hands. We have more than 80 million members. Almost 10,000 credit unions. More than 100,000 committed volunteers. Our management staff is trained and capable—and passionate. Our state and national leaders have vision and courage. We face serious challenges. But we are ready for the future.

I am deeply proud of my more than thirty years of service to the credit union movement. I am honored and humbled by this delicious award.

Thank you. Thank you. Thank you.

My Farewell

In the Classroom

I adored my credit union life. I loved being a professor at Pomona College. I announced a year in advance to both WCMS and Pomona College my intention to retire—I felt it was time. Everyone at WCMS was wonderful to me in the weeks and months of that last year. My WCMS board and colleagues were especially generous and supportive. I was touched that they endowed a generous student scholarship in my name at Pomona College.

When the time came I took home a few things from my office, and then my Economics Department kindly arranged for someone to come in and pack up all my books—thirty-two boxes worth—and transport them to a charity. I held on to my Carnegie Building office keys for about a week until Rhonda Beron, the Department administrator, asked for them. I was grieving.

But I have adapted—I am learning to embrace my retirement. At WCMS I look forward to attending Philosophy Night, joining the stage party in my cap and gown at Graduation, and meeting up with Alumni Association friends at their events all across the thirteen Western states served by WCMS. I also find pleasure in returning to the Economics Department to say hello or to sit in on a colloquium presentation.

I have a happy new life. I am fortunate to enjoy financial security, good friends, excellent health and a wonderful family.

There is a woman in my life—my wife, Chris—whom I love and who lets me know she loves me. She is a wonderful person. Chris and I are living our retirement in Claremont, California. Our children and their spouses are in their forties now, well-educated and in rewarding careers. They know we love them. We have been blessed with four granddaughters.

At the time I retired many of my former credit union colleagues and students reached out to me with expressions of thanks and love. Such a blessing. I feel deep gratitude for my life in credit unions.

At Home in Retirement

My Office at Pomona College: Carnegie Building;
See the two top-floor arched corner windows on left side of the photo

Jim and Chris

Remembrance

My deep participation in the world of credit unions was made possible by my four mentors. Steve Barden as education director of the California League taught me about credit unions, chaired the board of WCMS, and then paved the way for me to become a member of his credit union board when he himself became a credit union CEO. Dick Johnson of WesCorp, Bill Broxterman, President of the California Credit Union League, and David Chatfield who followed Broxterman as President of the California League, introduced me to the leaders of the movement on the national and international scenes. They made it possible for me to be culturally and politically aligned to the movement, yet able to participate as the independent voice of an academician.

Rick Craig and Diana Dykstra gave me important counsel about Western CUNA Management School from their vantage point as both faculty members and credit union system leaders.

Many people worked with me to assure the success of Western CUNA Management School. Charlie Clark was one of the school's founders and its director as I came on board. Each of the directors of education at the California Credit Union League worked with me over the years in a kind of provost role: Ginny Baldauf, Bill Sterner, Tom Vigueras, Donna Stone and Mark Klinkert took multi-year assignments. Bob Haage, Cheryl Haire, Chuck Harris and David Ellings became what would be the dean of students in a college. Donald Crawford—the brother I never had—lifted the soul of the place.

Molly Davis, Nancy Dotson, Diane Stewart and Nancy Wood each spent some years managing the business office side of the school.

Brandi Gleason and the many WCMS graduate assistants over the years provided essential leadership. Their compensation was only a dorm room and two weeks of dining hall food, unless one adds in the pride and self-respect that comes from making a significant difference in the lives of others.

WCMS has a visionary board of trustees, made up of influential credit union executives and I salute all the WCMS Trustees over the years. Patsy Von Ouwerkerk, Bill Cheney Darrin Williams, Brad Harvey, Teresa Freeborn, Shruti Miyashiro, Sterling Nielsen, Mark Klinkert, Scott Earl, Gene Pelham, Kevin Foster Keddie, Dianne Harding, Bernie Ray, Ava Milosovich, David Chatfield, Steve Barden, Vince Rojas, Fred Iverson, Damon Roemer, John Dulin, Barry Jolette, Troy Stang, Brett Martinez and Diana Dykstra.

The board of trustees' chairs were Steve Barden, Patsy VanOuwerkerk, Barry Jolette, Mary Cunningham, Shruti Miyashiro and Gene Pelham.

League Presidents across the thirteen states who supported WCMS included John Annaloro, Troy Stang, Carrol Beach, Tracie Kenyon, Scott Earl, Dennis Tanimoto, David Chatfield, Bill Cheney, Diana Dykstra, Scott Simpson, Sylvia Lyon and Kathy Thomson.

A committed alumni association, created under the leadership of intrepid Bob Toohey, provided invaluable backing.

Rick Craig and Diana Dykstra anchored the faculty. It importantly included Pomona College professors Martha Andresen, Kevin Dettmar, Michael Steinberger, Michael Kuehlwein, and Nicole Weekes. Other key instructors were Mario Conforti, Dick Heins, Dick Johnson, Joe Melchione, Stacy Hanke, Harry Eggleton, Matt Stephenson, Bill Birnie, Shruti Miyashiro, Bill Adler, Bruce Pearson, Bill Hampel, Michelle Bligh, Rudy Hanley, Gene Pelham, Mark Meyer, Neil Goldman and David Tansey. All were enormously significant and each deserves praise.

Kudos to Jan O'Neil, Pomona College's director of summer conferences over many years—a consummate professional—backed up by security, groundskeeper, maintenance, housekeeping and dining hall food-service workers, plus audio-visual support from the techies.

Lots of folks at the California League provided great assistance over the years. I am thinking in particular of Carol Payne, Joe Keller, Rich Silva, Natalie Moreno, Carmelita Keller, Tina Ramos-Ingold, Danielle Price, LaDonna Kohler, Matt Wrye, Cindy Tullues, Kevin Mann, Rita Fillingane, Jan Johnson, Angela Dailey and Rick Stanton.

I fondly remember the annual strategy meetings the WCMS management team had with our counterparts from the other CUNA management schools: Madison, Southeast and Southwest. Todd Spiczenski, Meghann Dawson, Amy Jesse, Joan Gillman, James Carrick, Janine McBee, Christina Lau, John Vardallas, Barbara Lehew-Bickley, Laura Parrish, Dan Denning and Tom McWilliams.

Thanks to Bill Hampel of CUNA for the many dual performances we did together. Credit unions were lucky to have had Bill Hampel.

Hank Dykstal, Marv Kilton and John Vardallas for many years included me in their CUNA conferences.

I remember Gene O'Rourke, Mike Sacher, Dan Moulton and the gang for the many years of pleasure, speaking at their conferences.

Hurrah to my colleagues at First City Credit Union over the years: Board, Management Supervisory Committee, and Staff. All of you, including Willa Glover, Barbara Oliver, Joe Milner, Bob Ciulik, Carrol Leonard, Marisa Lopez, John Benedict and Michael Steinberger from today's Board. And CEOs Jim Miller, Terry O'Steen, and Steve Punch. From long ago: Phil Pitts, Jack Preston, Chuck Miller, and Bruce Palmer.

Thank you to Kern Schools FCU for supporting my family over many years.

I especially appreciate the gifted Michael Steinberger, my Pomona College friend, colleague, and successor at WCMS.

Love always to my wife Chris and the kids, David, Elizabeth, Christopher, Andy, Gail, Norma and Shay, and to the grandkids Victoria, Lily, Kate and Caroline.

21207195R00052

Made in the USA
Lexington, KY
09 December 2018